DUNKIRK LITTLE SHIPS

Nigel Sharp

AMBERLEY

Cover images: Ray Little.

First published 2015

Amberley Publishing
The Hill, Stroud
Gloucestershire, GL5 4EP

www.amberley-books.com

Copyright © Nigel Sharp, 2015

The right of Nigel Sharp to be identified as the
Author of this work has been asserted in accordance
with the Copyrights, Designs and Patents Act 1988.

ISBN 978 1 4456 4750 0 (print)
ISBN 978 1 4456 4751 7 (ebook)

British Library Cataloguing in Publication Data.
A catalogue record for this book is available from
the British Library.

Typeset in 9.5pt on 12pt Celeste.
Typesetting by Amberley Publishing.
Printed in the UK.

Acknowledgements

With thanks to:

Ian Gilbert – Commodore of the Association of Dunkirk Little Ships
John Tough – Archivist of the Association of Dunkirk Little Ships
David Knight – Secretary of the Association of Dunkirk Little Ships
Christopher Thornhill – The Royal Cruising Club
The Bartlett Library, National Maritime Museum Cornwall
Heather Dennett – Michael Dennett Boat Builders
Ray Little
Tom Lee
Bruce Gordon-Smith
And everyone else who gave freely of information and images.

Introduction

On 10 May 1940, after eight months of relative inactivity between the warring armies in Europe, German troops began their invasion of Holland, Belgium and France. They advanced with astonishing speed, forcing the British Expeditionary Force and the French army to retreat to the coastal area of north-east France where, by 21 May, they were surrounded. At this time a plan was under consideration to evacuate Allied troops from three French ports, but a few days later German troops controlled two of them – Calais and Boulogne – and the only remaining option was Dunkirk.

At 18.57 on Sunday 26 May, the evacuation plan 'Operation Dynamo' was put into effect, but officials predicted that no more than 45,000 troops would be rescued during the three days that the Allies were expected to hold out.

However, a controversial German decision to call a temporary halt to their advance and a gallant rearguard action by Allied – but mostly French – troops allowed the evacuation to continue for nine days, during which 338,226 troops were evacuated. The fact that this was so many more than expected, even allowing for the longer timescale, was thanks to the mostly calm weather and to the huge fleet of vessels which had been hastily assembled, mostly from ports and rivers all over the south-east of England. Due to the very nature of the operation, nobody really knows how many boats took part, but it is generally thought to be in the region of 900, of which about 700 were privately owned.

Even at the start of the evacuation, enemy action had rendered much of Dunkirk harbour unusable, but it was still possible for ships to go alongside the East Mole, even though it was never intended for such a purpose and was only wide enough for troops to walk three-abreast along its 1,300-metre length. Nonetheless, it was from there that most of the troops – 239,555 of them – were evacuated. The remainder were taken off the gently shelving beaches stretching ten miles or so east of the harbour and across the Belgian border, typically by shallow-draught boats whose main role was to ferry them out to larger vessels waiting offshore. Around 200 of the vessels which went to Dunkirk didn't come back (including six destroyers) and a similar number were seriously damaged.

While many people now associate the term 'Dunkirk Little Ship' with the archetypal small cabin cruiser of the time, membership of the Association of Dunkirk Little Ships, which was formed soon after Operation Dynamo's twenty-fifth anniversary, is open to any type of non-service craft – including paddle steamers, tugs, barges, lifeboats, passenger ferries, fishing vessels and even a fireboat – which has survived, and to any service craft which is now in private ownership. Without the contribution of those Little Ships the numbers of troops rescued would have been far closer to the initial expectation, and there is little doubt that the outcome of the Second World War would have been fundamentally different.

German forces entered Calais several days before Dunkirk and, on the evening of 25 May, ten vessels were sent there to evacuate troops. *Conidaw* was one of these and the following morning she went in to Calais harbour and embarked 165 men, most of whom were wounded. However, almost as soon as she cast off she went aground on a falling tide and was a sitting target for German artillery for some five hours. Somehow she floated again when the tide came in and returned safely to Dover. Four days later, she crossed to Dunkirk and rescued another eighty soldiers. (Butch Dalrymple-Smith)

There were two other yachts in the Calais flotilla: the 35-metre *Grey Mist* and *Chico* (formerly *Blue Bird* – built 1932 and pictured here). Both came back to Dover empty-handed, however, as Allied forces were ordered to hold Calais at all costs and it was predominantly just the wounded who were evacuated. *Chico* then made two trips across to Dunkirk, transporting 217 troops back to Dover the first time, and then ferrying about 1,000 from the shore to waiting ships before bringing another 100 home. She was then assigned to 'life-saving' duties on one of the routes between Dover and Dunkirk. (G. L. Watson & Co. archive)

Royal Daffodil (built 1939) was one of ten vessels put on standby on 21 May when evacuations from the ports of Dunkirk, Calais and Boulogne were being considered. It is thought that during Operation Dynamo she made seven trips across the Channel and brought back up to 9,500 men, more than any other passenger vessel. On one trip a bomb passed straight through her and blew a hole in her hull just below the waterline, and it is said that it was plugged by a mattress. (Tom Lee Photostream)

At just 4.5 metres long, *Tamzine* (built 1937) is the smallest surviving Dunkirk Little Ship. Although many smaller boats took part, they would mostly have been taken there on board their mother ships, but *Tamzine* was towed there on her own bottom. She ferried troops from the beaches and then, whereas most vessels of her size were abandoned there, she was towed home by a Belgian trawler. She was exhibited at the London Boat Show in 1990 – the 50th anniversary year – and is now on display at the Imperial War Museum where she is pictured, somewhat poignantly, with a Spitfire in the background. (Nigel Sharp)

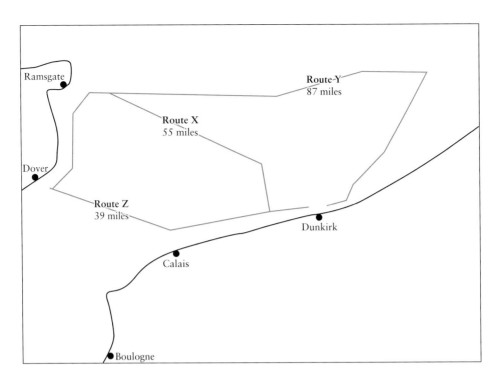

The shortest course from Dover to Dunkirk was 'Route Z', but as soon as the evacuation began it became apparent that this would be too dangerous, at least in daylight hours, due to the ease with which German troops could fire at passing Allied vessels from the Calais area. At that time the only alternative that avoided minefields and sandbanks was 'Route Y' but it was more than twice the distance, so during the course of 27 May, the new middle 'Route X' was created.

It was the Trinity House vessel *Patricia* (built 1938) that established and buoyed 'Route X', along with a destroyer and three minesweepers. When this work was completed, *Patricia's* tenders ferried troops out to her from the beaches and she brought them home. *Patricia* is now a restaurant in Stockholm while one of those tenders – now also called *Patricia* – is said to be undergoing a restoration. (Trinity House archive)

During the course of Operation Dynamo, *MTB102* (built 1937) made five trips to Dunkirk. Twice when returning to Dover she brought twenty soldiers back and several times she towed boatloads more from the beaches to outlying ships. She performed many other important duties, transporting various officials and delivering messages, but her most significant role began on 1 June. Rear Admiral Wake-Walker was in charge of directing Allied seagoing operations off Dunkirk, but when his flagship HMS *Keith* was considerably damaged in an air attack, he transferred to *MTB102* from which he continued his work for the remainder of the evacuation. However, as there was no Rear Admiral's flag on board, *MTB102*'s crew hastily made one from a dishcloth. The two photographs show her at her top speed of almost fifty knots in 1938 (when she had three 1,100 hp petrol engines) and at about twenty-seven knots in 2005 (with her two new 600 hp diesels). Her makeshift Rear Admiral's flag is inset. *MTB102* is the only surviving Royal Navy vessel which took part in Operation Dynamo, and is now based in Lowestoft. (Above: Vosper archive, inset: Richard Basey, below: MTB102 Trust/Nick Hall)

Laguna Belle (built 1896 and pictured here *c.* 1936) was one of more than twenty-three paddle steamers which took part in Operation Dynamo. (Tom Lee Photostream)

Crested Eagle (built 1925 and pictured here *c.* 1930) was one of six paddle steamers that never returned from Dunkirk. Immediately after leaving the East Mole with her complement of troops, she was hit by four bombs and caught fire. Although some men were rescued by other vessels, there were many casualties. (Tom Lee Photostream)

In common with most of the Dunkirk paddle steamers, *Princess Elizabeth* (built 1927) had been serving as a minesweeper since the beginning of the war and was initially sent over to Dunkirk in that capacity, but she subsequently brought back a total of 1,673 soldiers in four trips, all of them from the beaches. She is one of just two surviving Operation Dynamo paddle steamers and she is now a tourism and conference centre in the town of Dunkirk. (ADLS archive)

Gracie Fields (built 1936 and pictured here the following year) is also at Dunkirk today, but as a wreck on the beaches. Having brought 281 troops safely back to Dover, she went back the next day and loaded 750 more. However, she was bombed soon afterwards and the resulting damage to her engines and steering caused her to circle uncontrollably. Amazingly, various other vessels managed to get alongside and transfer all the soldiers and the crew before she sank. Ironically, during the early part of the First World War, she had taken more than half a million soldiers over to France. (Tom Lee Photostream)

L'Orage (formerly *Surrey* – built 1938) was purchased by the television personality Raymond Baxter in the spring of 1964. A few months later, aware that it would be the 25th anniversary of the Dunkirk evacuation the following year, he asked the *Sunday Times* – whose editor, Dennis Hamilton, had been rescued from the beaches – to publish a letter saying he planned to take *L'Orage* to Dunkirk to mark the anniversary, and asking if anyone else was interested in doing so. As a result of this, fifty-five boats – not all of which had taken part in the evacuation – crossed to Dunkirk in 1965 accompanied by vessels from the Royal Navy and the RNLI. The top photograph shows some of those boats crossing the Channel in 1965 (ADLS archive) and the bottom photograph shows *L'Orage* in 2010. (Ray Little)

As a result of discussions soon after the 1965 Return, the Association of Dunkirk Little Ships was formed. Members are entitled to fly the Association's House Flag, which is the Cross of St George defaced with the Arms of Dunkirk (pictured here) and, when in company with other Little Ships, they can also fly the undefaced Cross of St George at the bow. (John Tough)

Dunkirk Little Ships are also entitled to display a plaque with 'DUNKIRK 1940' marked on it. This one belongs to *L'Orage*. (Ray Little)

At the request of the Ministry of Shipping, Doug Tough, of Teddington boatbuilders Tough Brothers, assembled a fleet of about a hundred vessels at his yard just as Operation Dynamo was getting under way. Doug's team then prepared them all for the task ahead by ensuring they were in working order and stripping out their cabins to create as much space inside them as possible, while documenting everything that was removed. That fleet included *Lamouette* (built 1937) and *Smolt* (built 1936). After the evacuation, Doug spent two months searching for surviving boats, gathering them at Sheerness and then towing them back up the Thames. There were six such tows in all, one of them comprising *Lamouette*, *Smolt* and seventeen others. The Admiralty later officially stated that the hundred boats which had been assembled at Teddington were responsible for bringing home between 3,000 and 5,000 soldiers. Doug Tough's son Bob was Commodore of the ADLS from 1986 to 1987 and his grandson John has been the ADLS Archivist since 2001. *Above*: *Lamouette*. (ADLS archive) *Below*: *Smolt*. (ADLS archive)

Janthea (formerly *Reda* – built 1938) was also made ready for the Dunkirk evacuation at Teddington. While she was there, her owner, a publican, briefly called in and suggested that the well-stocked drinks locker should be left that way as 'the chaps will have a greater need for it than me'. She crossed to Dunkirk twice: the first time she brought twenty-one men home, and then she ferried fifty French troops to off-lying ships before bringing twenty-three more back to Ramsgate. (Ray Little)

Angele Aline (built 1921) was on her way from Saint-Valery-en-Caux, where a new propeller had been fitted, back to her home port of Nieuport when she was commandeered to assist in the evacuation. Nothing is known of the part she played, but the next year she was sunk by British aircraft while fishing off Saint-Vaast-la-Hougue. She was later refloated and in 1943 the Germans used her to blockade the entrance to Nieuport harbour. (Ray Little)

Following the 1965 Return, another was planned for 1970. Unfortunately it was cancelled due to bad weather, but since then further Returns have taken place every five years. The record was set in 1990 when seventy-five Little Ships commemorated the 50th anniversary. These photographs are of *Wendy Ken* (formerly *Sylvia* – built 1930) and were taken during the 1965 (above, ADLS archive) and 2000 (below, Ray Little) Returns. *Wendy Ken* made two trips to Dunkirk in 1940. The Ramsgate harbourmaster later reported that when she came back the first time she had a hole just above the waterline which the troops she was carrying had plugged with their coats, and when she finally arrived home she was on the verge of sinking.

Tahilla and *Greta* taking part in the 2000 Return. During Operation Dynamo, *Tahilla* (formerly *Skylark* – built 1922) was abandoned after her steering was damaged when she was hit by enemy fire. She was later found drifting off Dunkirk and was towed back by *Southern Queen*. (Ray Little)

Aberdonia (built 1935) following *Janthea* and other Little Ships while a Spitfire flies overhead during the 2000 Return. (Ray Little)

The Thames sailing barge *Greta* (built 1892) was one of thirty or more barges that went to Dunkirk in 1940. About a third of them failed to return, but this is largely because they were deliberately beached so that their cargo of water, food and ammunition would be accessible to waiting troops. *Greta* is still sailing today, offering charters from her base in Whitstable. The bottom photograph shows her arriving at Dunkirk for the 2005 Return. (Above: ADLS archive, below: Ray Little)

The London fireboat *Massey Shaw* (built 1935) made three trips to Dunkirk, initially with a view to fire fighting, but when that became impractical she began to rescue troops. She helped to ferry about 500 out to waiting ships and brought 106 more back to Ramsgate. She was then ordered back to London, but soon after she set off she went to the aid of a nearby French ship, which had struck a mine and was sinking fast. The *Massey Shaw* picked up forty severely injured men and subsequently transferred them to another vessel. She is now owned by the Massey Shaw and Marine Vessels Preservation Society. A major restoration was completed in 2013 – thanks, in part, to a Heritage Lottery Fund grant – and she is thought to be the oldest operating fireboat in Europe. She was never meant to go to sea – or at least not after she completed her delivery voyage from her builder's yard in Cowes in 1935 – but not only did she make it across the Channel three times in 1940, she has also been on three Returns. These photographs show her in her home waters of the Thames (above, Ambrose Greenway) and on the 2000 Return (below, Ray Little).

Nineteen RNLI lifeboats, from every station between Bournemouth, where *Thomas Kirk Wright* (built 1938) was based, to Great Yarmouth, went to Dunkirk. *Thomas Kirk Wright* was particularly suited to getting close in to the Dunkirk beaches because she had a revolutionary propulsion system without vulnerable propellers. She made three trips across and on one of them came under fire from German troops, as a result of which one engine was disabled and she took in a lot of water. These photographs show her on a callout in her very early days (above, Andrew Hawkes Poole archive), and in Poole Harbour in the hands of Phil Neate, her owner for ten years after she came out of service in 1964 (below, Brian Traves collection). She is now a static display in Poole Lifeboat Museum.

Michael Stephens (built 1939) was the Lowestoft lifeboat. She was accidentally rammed by two Allied Motor Torpedo Boats (MTBs) and a fishing boat in the process of ferrying twelve French troops out to off-lying ships and then bringing fifty-two more back to Dover. She was originally paid for by the same legacy as the *Louise Stephens*, the Great Yarmouth lifeboat, which brought forty-nine soldiers back to Ramsgate. (Paul Richards)

Abdy Beauclerk (built 1931) and *Lucy Lavers* (built 1940) were both stationed at Aldeburgh. *Lucy Lavers* had only just arrived from her builder's yard when she was commandeered for Operation Dynamo. Both boats were towed across to Dunkirk – a common occurrence, for speed and to conserve fuel – and then ferried men from the beaches and harbour out to waiting ships. This photograph shows her responding to a later peacetime callout, while *Abdy Beauclerk* remains on the beach behind her. She is now being restored by Rescue Wooden Boats. (Maurice Smith)

Mark and Penny Webb have owned *Firefly* (built 1923) since 2013 and keep her at Swale Marina in Kent. Denis Kinnell spent two days waiting on the beaches in 1940 before being brought home by *Firefly*, and the bottom photograph shows him on board again (middle), at the 2000 Return with her then-owners. (Above: Mark Webb, below: Mark Webb collection)

A Spitfire Mk IXB flies over the Little Ships during the 2000 Return. (Ray Little)

Three spectacular boats taking part in the 2000 Return, all designed as 'gentlemen's motor yachts' by legendary British designers and built in the 1930s: *Atlantide* (formerly *Caleta*) – designed by Alfred Mylne and built by Philip & Son in Dartmouth; *Bounty* – designed by Charles E. Nicholson and built by Camper & Nicholsons in Gosport; *Blue Bird of 1938* – designed by G. L. Watson and built by Goole Shipbuilding Co. All three were requisitioned for service throughout most of the Second World War. (Ray Little)

P.S. Brighton Belle.

Brighton Belle (built 1900 and pictured here *c.* 1930) was another paddle steamer which was lost during Operation Dynamo. With 800 troops on board, she hit the submerged wreck of another vessel which had struck a mine just a few hours earlier, and started to sink rapidly. Other vessels, including the paddle steamers *Sandown* and *Medway Queen*, quickly came alongside and were able to rescue everyone, including the captain's dog. (Tom Lee Photostream, inset: Eric Woodroffe)

Sandown (built 1934 and pictured here *c.* 1960) already had her own dog, a dachshund called Bombproof Bella that proved to be a particularly lucky mascot. During three trips to Dunkirk, *Sandown* was relentlessly attacked from the land and the air and came through unscathed, bringing home 1,861 troops. (Tom Lee Photostream)

The Dunkirk record of *Medway Queen* (built 1924) is remarkable. She was one of the first vessels to go across and one of the last to come back, making seven trips in total, some to the beaches and others to the harbour. She is thought to have brought almost 7,000 men back to Dover and Ramsgate, including the survivors of the *Brighton Belle*. Her crew shot down three enemy aircraft. Although she came very close to being broken up in the early 1960s, she still survives today and, thanks to a Heritage Lottery Fund grant, she has been undergoing an extensive restoration. After her hull was rebuilt in Bristol, in November 2013 she was towed through Clifton Gorge (see photograph) to Gillingham for the restoration to continue. It is hoped she will soon be back in full working order. (Above: Richard Halton collection, below: Bob Stokes)

THAMES QUEEN

Thames Queen (pictured here *c.* 1935) had not only been serving as a minesweeper since the beginning of the Second World War, but had also performed the same role in the First World War. (Tom Lee Photostream)

Pleasure Steamer at Pier, Bournemouth

Emperor of India (built 1906) served as a hospital ship, troop carrier and minesweeper in the First World War, as far afield as the eastern Mediterranean. She is thought to have made three trips to Dunkirk, bringing a total of 642 troops back to Dover. (Tom Lee Photostream)

Nothing is known about the Dunkirk service of *Thamesa* (formerly *Minnehaha* and *Tigris III* – built 1936) but Doug Tough found her with a badly burnt wheelhouse in Ramsgate afterwards. He took her back to Teddington and removed the aft coachroof so that he could use her as a tug, but he refitted it when he bought her for his personal use in 1944. She has been in the Tough family ever since and is now owned by John Tough, the ADLS Archivist. She once transported the Beatles to Thames Television studios to avoid crowds of obsessive fans and she also conveyed a petition to Parliament to protest about the imposition of 25 per cent VAT on boats in 1975. These photographs show her as *Tigris III* in 1943 at Teddington, where she is still kept today (ADLS archive), and in Dunkirk harbour in 2010 (Ville de Dunkerque).

Mimosa (built 1935) and *Greta* in Ramsgate at dawn on the day of the 2005 Return. (Ray Little)

Wairakei II following *Riis I* on the 2005 Return. *Riis I* (formerly *White Heather* – built 1920) had petrol/paraffin engines in 1940 and they let her down twice during Operation Dynamo. She broke down while she was leading a convoy of eight boats from Sheerness to Ramsgate, and was taken in tow; after repairs were carried out, she crossed the Channel but was later found deserted and at anchor after her engines had failed again. She was eventually towed home. (Ray Little)

Fedalma II and *Princess Freda* on the 2005 Return. (Ray Little)

Part of the fleet of fifty-four Little Ships on their way to Dunkirk for the 2005 Return. (Ray Little)

By the time *Maid Marion* (built 1925) set off from her home port of Porthleven, Cornwall, she was too late to take part in Operation Dynamo. However, about a week later she brought soldiers home from Le Havre during Operation Cycle, and as such is entitled to membership of the ADLS. She has been owned by David Hunt and kept on the River Deben since 1965. These photographs show her in Porthleven in the 1950s (above, David Hunt collection) and on the 2005 Return with *HMS Severn* (below, Ray Little).

In May 1940 *Makaira* (formerly *113RFC* – built 1938) was in Jersey, where it was planned to establish an Air Sea Rescue base. Engine trouble prevented her from going to Dunkirk but she played an active part in Operation Aerial, the evacuation of Saint-Malo (and so is also entitled to membership of the ADLS). Twice she went there, the first time to evacuate RAF personnel and civilians, and then to collect the BEF demolition party, leaving just as German forces were entering the town. Jon Blair bought her in 2012 and has had extensive work done to her at Michael Dennett Boat Builders. (Beken)

Among the fleet of boats that took part in Operation Aerial were eighteen belonging to members of St Helier Yacht Club. They were taken to Saint-Malo by their owners and friends, and they helped to rescue 21,474 Allied troops. One of them was *Girl Joyce*, seen here sailing in Saint Aubin's Bay, Jersey, in 2010. (Kevin le Scelleur)

It is thought that *Southern Queen* (built 1927) made three trips over to Dunkirk, and on each occasion spent the night ferrying troops from the East Mole to waiting ships. She eventually towed one of the Eastbourne lifeboats and the yacht *Skylark* (now *Tahilla*) back to Dover. (ADLS archive)

Singapore II (built 1937) was commandeered for Operation Dynamo but never made it across the Channel as her engine failed. Things went from bad to worse when the tow tore out part of her foredeck but she was eventually returned to Ramsgate. However, *Singapore II* still qualifies for membership of the ADLS, as do all boats that were commandeered for operations Dynamo, Cycle and Aerial, whether they made it across or not. Engine breakdowns were fairly common, but some boats stayed in home ports in supporting roles while others were simply commandeered too late. (ADLS archive)

Over 160 fishing vessels took part in Operation Dynamo. *Enterprise* (built 1912) and *Edward and Mary* (built 1919) were two of a dozen or so from Hastings which were ordered to report to Dover, but they never crossed the Channel, probably because by that time the Germans were overrunning the town and only boats capable of speeds of twenty knots were sent over. The photograph of *Enterprise* shows her in Hastings Fishermen's Museum while *Edward and Mary* – pictured in 1947 – is now on display on the beach outside the museum. (Steve Peak collection)

Planes of the Battle of Britain Memorial Flight flying over various Little Ships during the 2000 Return. (Ray Little)

Challenge, MTB102 and others on the 2005 Return. (Ray Little)

Glala, Fedalma II, Wairakei II, Princess Freda, Tahilla and *MTB102* (left to right) on the 2005 Return. (Ray Little)

Silver Queen (formerly *Fermain V* – built 1926) was reported to have been sunk during Operation Dynamo, but she was later refloated and brought home. The photograph shows her as *Fermain V* in company with HMS *Somerset* on the 2000 Return, but she has since been given her original name again. (Ray Little)

Princess Freda (built 1926) and *Jeff* (built 1923) were both Thames passenger launches before they took part in Operation Dynamo, and they still are today. They crossed to Dunkirk together in a flotilla of similar vessels and ferried troops from the beaches to outlying ships. Both were disabled when their propellers were either damaged or fouled – a huge problem for many vessels throughout the evacuation with so much debris in the water – as a result of which *Princess Freda* was towed home by the Dutch tug *Betje* while *Jeff* was abandoned. She was later rescued, however, and brought home by French soldiers, but her sister ship *Mutt* was lost. *Princess Freda* (top, Ray Little) has been owned by the Collier family since 2000 and is based at Westminster, while the Turk family has had *Jeff* (bottom, The Turk collection) for over forty years and operate her between Richmond and Hampton Court.

Hilfranor (built 1935) was abandoned at Dunkirk after sustaining damage in an attack by German dive bombers. It is said that she was later found by some desperate French soldiers just as German troops were arriving, and they brought her back across the Channel. The crew of a minesweeper subsequently saw her sinking near the Goodwin Sands and towed her into Ramsgate. She is now owned by Simon Palmer, the Vice Commodore of the ADLS. (Ian Gilbert)

Fedalma II (built 1936) was owned by John Knight, the first ADLS Archivist, for many years. His family sold her to David Johnson-Biggs in the late 1990s and he now keeps her at Woodbridge. (Ray Little)

Blue Bird of 1938 (formerly *Blue Bird* – built 1938) was the third yacht of the same name – all of which were at Dunkirk – built for Sir Malcolm Campbell, the holder of various land and water speed records. These photographs were taken during her initial sea trials in 1938, almost certainly on the Humber, and in 2007 in Saint Tropez after an extensive restoration. The war ended Campbell's dream to take *Blue Bird* treasure hunting in the Pacific Cocos Islands but her current owner, Tara Getty, plans to take her there in 2015 as part of a world cruise. (G. L. Watson & Co. archive)

Atlantide (formerly *Caleta* – built 1930) came under heavy attack during her day at Dunkirk and was also involved in a collision with the yacht *Bounty*. She was still able to assist various other vessels, one of which was a landing craft from which she transferred thirty-five troops before towing it back to Sheerness, where she disembarked the men. *Atlantide* was gloriously restored in the late 1990s and is now owned by Leslie and Rick Fairbanks, who keep her in the USA. These photographs show her motor-sailing during the 2000 Return (above, Ray Little) and in Norway in 2008 (below, Justin Christou).

Fedalma II leads a group of Little Ships on the 2005 Return. (Ray Little)

Stenoa follows other Little Ships during the 2005 Return. (Ray Little)

Fedalma II follows other Little Ships on the 2005 Return. (Ray Little)

Chico, shown here taking part in the 2005 Return. She is now a charter vessel operating in Scotland. (Ray Little)

As Holland was falling to the Germans, a fortnight before the Dunkirk evacuation, large numbers of Dutch Schuits (or Skoots, self-propelled barges in all shapes and sizes) crossed over to England. Around forty of them took part in Operation Dynamo and four were lost. It is thought that just two survive today, one being *Welsh Liberty* (formally *Amazone* – built 1936) which made three trips across to Dunkirk, bringing a total of 549 troops back to Dover and Ramsgate. In early 2015 she was for sale in France. (Roosens Marine Group)

Bounty (built 1936) on the 2000 Return. During part of Operation Dynamo, Commodore Stephenson (who was in charge of operations in one particular area off the beaches) used *Bounty* as his flagship, and she also transported Lord Gort (Commander-in-Chief of the BEF) from one destroyer to another. Furthermore, she ferried about 1,000 men out to off-lying ships before bringing 150 more back to Ramsgate, albeit under tow after she fouled her propeller. (Ray Little)

Blue Bird of Chelsea (formerly *Bluebird* – built 1931) was towed to Dunkirk in 1940 by the paddle steamer *Emperor of India*. This was probably to conserve her fuel to use on the other side, so it was ironic that her engines then failed when water was poured into her fuel tanks – a common problem because petrol cans were used to transport water to the waiting troops as there was a shortage of water containers. Furthermore, her propellers were fouled by some debris in the water, and she was towed home by the Dutch Schuit *Hilda* empty handed. (Ray Little)

Gentle Ladye (formerly *Jong* – built 1931) was known to have taken thirteen troops out to a Dutch Schuit and then continued to ferry more until she and some nearby boats came under air attack. She assisted in towing other vessels until she herself developed engine trouble and was towed home by a drifter. (ADLS archive)

The Little Ships gather in Ramsgate for the 2010 Return. Dover has been used as the starting or finishing port for some other Returns. (Ray Little)

The three Little Ships in the foreground – among others gathering in Ramsgate the day before setting off to Dunkirk for the 2010 Return – illustrate the variety of vessels which took part in Operation Dynamo: the gentlemen's motor yacht *Bounty*; the 1892 Thames barge *Greta*; and the Motor Torpedo Boat *MTB102*. (Ray Little)

The Returns always attract enthusiastic crowds on both sides of the Channel, whatever the weather. These 2010 photographs show *Mimosa* leaving Ramsgate, and *Elvin*, *Margo II*, *Hilfranor* and others arriving in Dunkirk later the same day. (Above: Ray Little, below: Ville de Dunkerque)

These photographs show *Naiad Errant* (built 1939) on the River Thames soon after she was launched in 1939, and passing the end of Dunkirk's East Mole during the 1990 Return. It can be seen from the second photograph that the East Mole was never designed for vessels to go alongside and why it was essential that troops should also be ferried by shallow-draught vessels – such as *Naiad Errant* – from the beaches out to waiting ships. Before *Naiad Errant* got to the beaches she rescued twenty survivors from the French destroyer *Foudroyant*, which had been sunk by enemy aircraft, and transferred them to a tug. She then went aground while ferrying men from the beaches and was abandoned. About four hours later she refloated and her original crew reboarded her along with nine troops, but soon after that both engines failed, probably due to the same petrol container confusion experienced by *Blue Bird of Chelsea*. One engine was eventually restarted and *Naiad Errant* motored slowly back to Ramsgate. The number seven on her bows is a nostalgic throwback to her time as a harbour patrol launch in Felixstowe later in the war. (Hugh Collinson collection)

Aquabelle (built 1939) is known to have towed five other vessels back from Dunkirk. This photograph shows her on her delivery voyage from her builders in Littlehampton to Hampton Wick on the Thames. She is now co-owned by her original owner's grandson, Colin Dimbylow, and a Frenchman who is organising a team of volunteers to restore her in the Mediterranean. (Colin Dimbylow collection)

Mada (formerly *Fleury II* – built 1936) has been owned by Stephen Dargavel since 2010 and she is kept at Marlow. (Stephen Dargavel collection)

C. H. Lightoller was the most senior officer to survive the sinking of the *Titanic*. He took his own boat *Sundowner* (built 1912) to Dunkirk, although it was unusual for owners to do so. On the way across he rescued five men from the yacht *Westerly*, which had caught fire. He then took *Sundowner* alongside a destroyer on the East Mole and embarked 122 troops. On the way back to Ramsgate they were attacked by enemy aircraft and Lightoller found that evasive techniques previously explained to him by his son, an RAF pilot, were extremely effective.

Ramsgate played a significant part in *Sundowner's* life again, when she arrived there in a storm in 1986. She was in poor condition and her owners didn't have the funds to carry out the necessary work, so a local boatyard suggested cutting her up with a chainsaw. Luckily John Knight, at that time Archivist of the ADLS, happened to be in Ramsgate sheltering from the same storm on his own Little Ship *Fedalma* and heard about the impending disaster and managed to prevent it. These photographs show her at West Mersea in 1942 (above, Jim Harris collection) and on the Thames in 2012 (below, ADLS archive).

Chumley (formerly *Chalmondesleigh* – built 1934) was owned by the comedian Tommy Trinder when she went to Dunkirk. She originally had a cabin, but when she fell into a state of disrepair sometime after the war she was restored as an open launch. Roy and Sally Hamilton bought her in 2010 and decided to reinstate her cabin. These photos show her before and after her latest conversion: on the 2010 Return (above, with *Riis II* and *Tahilla*, Ray Little) and between Chatham and Ramsgate in 2014 (below, Alex Ramsey), illustrating how fortunate it was that the weather for most of the nine days of Operation Dynamo was calm.

Amazone (formerly *Mermaiden*) and *Lijns*, pictured here taking part in the 2010 Return, were both built in steel at the same yard, de Vries in Holland, in 1939 and 1934 respectively. *Lijns* has been owned by the Tolhurst family since 1988. They found her in a poor state on the River Medway and did a great deal of work to her just in time for the 1990 Return, and have taken her to every Return since. (Ray Little)

Aureol, L'Orage, Ryegate II, Wanda, Chumley, Margo II and *Lady Gay* on the 2010 Return. *Margo II* (built 1931) was purchased by David Knight, the Secretary of the ADLS, in 2014; *Lady Gay* (built 1934) has been owned by Jason Carley and his family since 2008 and is based at Hampton Court. (Ray Little)

This photograph shows twelve of the forty-eight boats that took part in the 2010 Return. (Ray Little)

Angele Aline follows *Stenoa* and other Little Ships on the 2010 Return. (Ray Little)

Elvin (built 1937) went alongside Dunkirk's East Mole at dawn on 2 June and embarked twenty-five French and eight British troops, intending to transfer them to a larger vessel to bring them home. However, all attempts to find such a vessel failed so, despite being considerably overloaded, *Elvin* brought them safely back to Ramsgate. She is now owned by Hywel and Jane Bowen-Perkins, who keep her at Hampton on the Thames. (Derek May)

Constant Nymph, pictured here outside Twickenham Yacht Club in the late 1930s, was another boat that was taken to Dunkirk by her owner, Dr B. A. Smith. She spent a night over there working with a cutter and a whaler, ferrying about 900 soldiers to the Dutch motor vessels *Jutland* and *Laudania*. As dawn came *Constant Nymph's* engine started to play up, so Smith and his crew were ordered aboard *Laudania*, which then set off for home while Smith's little boat was assigned to a naval drifter. (ADLS archive)

In 1941, the Cruising Club of America decided to award its coveted Blue Water Medal to the amateur yachtsmen who took part in the evacuation of Dunkirk. The US Naval Attaché presented it to the Vice Commodore of the Royal Cruising Club at a ceremony in Lincoln's Inn. The medal is still on display in the RCC's club room in Knightsbridge, while the Little Ship Club (established in 1926, its name should not be confused with the Dunkirk Little Ships) and the Royal Ocean Racing Club have replicas. (Nigel Sharp)

Windsong (built 1931) was one of at least five David Hillyard-built sailing boats to take part in Operation Dynamo. She made two trips to Dunkirk, the first under the command of her owner, G. L. Dalton. She was recently thought to be based in the eastern Mediterranean. (ADLS archive)

Devon Belle, Janthea, Wairakei II and *Iorana* follow other Little Ships on the 2010 Return.
(Ray Little)

Fermain V (now *Silver Queen*) and *Hilfranor,* escorted by HMS *Monmouth* during the 2010 return.
(ADLS archive)

Amazone went over to Dunkirk three times in 1940. The third time, she was towed there and back by the tug *Sun IV*, but while she was there she made four trips from the harbour to waiting ships while coming under fire from German troops entering the town. It is said that her superstructure was riddled with bullets and that she was so crowded that her skipper couldn't see to steer, and instructions had to be shouted by someone who could. She is pictured here leading other Little Ships over to Dunkirk for the 2010 Return. (Ray Little)

Hilfranor following other Little Ships on the 2010 return. (ADLS archive)

Queen of Thanet (built 1916 and pictured here *c.* 1935) made four crossings to Dunkirk and brought 2,500 troops back to Margate. 2,000 more were transferred to her when she went alongside the considerably larger vessel *Prague* – which was sinking as a result of Luftwaffe attacks – while both vessels were travelling at full speed. (Tom Lee Photostream)

Oriole (formerly *Eagle III* – built 1910) made five trips to Dunkirk. When she arrived there the first time, her captain deliberately beached her because he could see that the small boats involved in transferring operations were having difficulties. This allowed more than 2,000 men to climb across her decks to board other vessels and when she refloated at the next high tide she was able to bring 700 more home. She repeated the operation the next day, but on subsequent visits she went into Dunkirk harbour. Official reports say she transported 2,587 troops, but her captain thought it was closer to 5,000. (Tom Lee Photostream)

GOLDEN EAGLE.   A. R. R.

In three trips to Dunkirk, *Golden Eagle* (built 1903 and pictured here *c.* 1912) brought back 1,751 men. On her second trip, she helped to rescue survivors from the paddle steamer *Waverley*, which had been hit by three bombs dropped by the Luftwaffe. (Tom Lee Photostream)

Eight of the Isle of Man Steam Packet Company's passenger vessels took part in Operation Dynamo, and they are credited with bringing home 24,699 troops. However, in a twenty-four-hour period three of them were lost, including *Mona's Queen* which, having already brought about 1,200 men safely home, hit a mine and sank within two minutes when she went across a second time. Thirty-two survivors were rescued. In 2010 her anchor was raised and returned to the Isle of Man, and is now the focal point of a memorial at Port St Mary that honours the Company's employees who served in the war. (Isle of Man Steam Packet Company archive)

Trimilia (formerly *Prudential* – built 1925) was the Ramsgate lifeboat and was one of only two – the other being *Lord Southborough*, the Margate boat – which was taken to Dunkirk by her regular RNLI volunteer crew. Initially, she towed eight other vessels, mostly wherries with fresh water supplies for the waiting troops, across to the beaches. She then helped to ferry more than 2,000 men out to waiting ships. David and Moira Jay bought her in 2005 and now keep her in Ipswich. (David Jay collection)

Dowager (formerly the lifeboat *Rosa Wood and Phyllis Lunn* – built 1932) was based at Shoreham and it is thought that she made two, maybe three, trips across, collecting troops from both the beaches and the harbour. (ADLS archive)

Stenoa (formerly *Cecil and Lilian Philpott* – built 1930) was the Newhaven lifeboat that brought fifty-one soldiers home. She is pictured here taking part in the 2005 Return. (Ray Little)

Mary Scott (built 1925) was the Southwold lifeboat. In 1940 she was towed over to Dunkirk by the *Emperor of India* along with two other small boats, and the three of them then worked together to take 210 men out to off-lying ships. Her crew abandoned her and came home in another lifeboat when her engine failed, but others later restarted it and brought her home. She is pictured here taking part in the 2010 Return. (ADLS archive)

Seven Little Ships that were all built in timber in the 1930s: *L'Orage* leading (left to right) *Mada*, *Janthea*, *Margo II*, *Lazy Days*, *Chumley* and *Wanda* back from the 2010 Return. (Ray Little)

Wairakei II, followed by the former lifeboats *Stenoa* and *Dowager*, taking part in the wreath-laying ceremony during the 2010 Return. (Ray Little)

Mada (obscuring *Lady Gay*), *Wanda* (slightly obscuring *Ryegate II*), *Margo II* and *Aureol* on the 2010 Return. (Ray Little)

Wanda and *Mada,* both of which were built by Elkins of Christchurch, in 1935 and 1936 respectively, arriving back in Ramsgate after the 2010 Return with *Lazy Days* and others close behind. (Ray Little)

MB278 (built 1914) was lucky to make it to the start of Operation Dynamo. Built as a naval pinnace early in the First World War, her mothership was sunk in the Aegean Sea in 1918 but somehow *MB278* survived. In March 1940, she sank when she was crushed in Portsmouth harbour, but was raised and hastily repaired. Michael and Stephen Dennett acquired her in 2010 and have extensively restored her, finding some seventy-year-old bullet holes in her hull in the process. These two photographs show her in contrasting conditions: the top one was taken on the way to Ramsgate to take part in the 2010 Return, and is another illustration of why Allied forces were so lucky to have had such calm conditions for most of the nine days of the evacuation. (Above: Jason Carley, below: Heather Dennett)

Endeavour (built 1926) was one of six Leigh-on-Sea Cockle Bawley boats which took part in Operation Dynamo. As they approached Dunkirk in convoy they were attacked by about forty German planes, but they escaped harm by steering deliberately erratic courses. Between them they transferred about 1,000 men from the outside of the East Mole and the inside of the harbour to waiting ships, and then brought 180 more back to Ramsgate. Another cockle boat, the *Renown*, was blown to pieces by a mine, killing her three crew. These two photographs show *Endeavour* racing at Leigh-on-Sea regatta in 1938 (above, with *Resolute*, another Dunkirk cockle boat, just behind); and after a restoration carried out by the Leigh-on-Sea Endeavour Trust in the 2000s (below). (Leigh-on-Sea Endeavour Trust archive)

Anne (built 1925) leaving Ramsgate for the 2010 Return. She is thought to be the only Little Ship to go to Dunkirk that year with her original engines – a pair of Ailsa Craig petrol/paraffin LB4s. (Ray Little)

Ferry Nymph was based in Poole Harbour, ferrying passengers across the harbour entrance, when she was commandeered to take part in Operation Dynamo. From Dover she crossed to Dunkirk and brought 162 troops back to Ramsgate in two trips. She is pictured here taking part in the 2010 Return. (ADLS archive)

Mary Jane (built 1926) has been owned by Samantha Kennedy and Travis Van Moorsel since 2012. They keep her at South Dock Marina, Surrey Quays. She is pictured here arriving in Dunkirk for the 2010 Return. (Ray Little)

Princess Freda, Riis II, Elvin, MB278 and *Mada* in Dunkirk for the 2010 Return. (ADLS archive)

Pudge (built 1922) and two other barges were towed over to Dunkirk in 1940 by the tug *St Fagan*. When they arrived on the other side, soon after the tow was released *St Fagan* hit a mine and was destroyed, along with the two other barges. Somehow *Pudge* survived and was able to pick up survivors, although there were only six from *St Fagan's* twenty-five-man crew. Soon afterwards, *Pudge* was towed back to Ramsgate by the tug *Tanga*. She is one of just four surviving Thames barges that took part in Operation Dynamo. (Thames Sailing Barge Trust archive)

The *Viscountess Wakefield* was the only RNLI lifeboat to be lost at Dunkirk, but for a while the *Capitan Eduardo Simpson Roth* (formerly *E.M.E.D.*, the Walton-on-the-Naze boat – built 1928) was thought to be. On her first trip across the naval officer in charge of her was killed when she came under fire and she was later found with a rope around her propeller. She was towed home before going over a second time and bringing thirty-nine troops back. She was sold out of service to Chile in 1956 and is still in use with Chilean Lifeboat Society in Valparaiso, where she is pictured in 2010. (Mike Waddleton)

Len Jones bought *Aureol* (formerly *Kitty* – built 1936) in 1979 and she is now owned by his son Simon. Soon after setting off from Dover for the 1985 Return her engine broke down, but she has made it to Dunkirk for every Return since, and is pictured here on her way to Ramsgate for the beginning of the event in 2010. She is kept at Weybridge on the River Thames. (Simon Palmer)

Nyula (built 1933) has attended every Return since 1985. Alex Ramsey bought her in 2005 and he keeps her on the River Soar in Leicestershire. (John Hoskins)

The Little Ships that came home from Dunkirk must have had a certain amount of luck. However, those that are still around today – the vast majority of which have, at some point, fallen into a state of disrepair – also owe their ongoing survival to their owners' dedication, enthusiasm and hard work, all qualities which tend to be enhanced simply because of the Little Ships' unique history. This photograph shows the former RNLI lifeboat the *Cyril and Lilian Bishop* about to be restored by Evans Marine International in France. (Evans Marine International archive)

Lazy Days pictured during her extensive restoration at Classic Restoration Services in 2014. It was initially thought that she just needed new decks and her hull painted but, as is so often the case, further inspection revealed that her problems went much deeper. Apart from the new decks, about 45 per cent of her hull planking, all the steamed timbers and the wheelhouse were also renewed, as were her engines. (The Finn collection)

Elsa II (built 1929) was purchased in 2013 by Chris Brightman and Shelley Price, who 'fell in love with her and her beautiful shape and decided to rescue her and bring her back to her former glory'. They were 'also excited about being able to take part in the restoration of a little part of history'. She is pictured here just as her restoration at Michael Dennett Boat Builders was about to get under way. (Dennetts Boat Builders archive)

While many of the Little Ships that have survived are small enough for enthusiastic private owners to expend the time and money needed to ensure their survival, some vessels are just too big, and it has been necessary to set up trusts and other organisations. This photograph shows the *Medway Queen* abandoned in the Medina River in 1980. Four years later she was re-floated, loaded onto a salvage pontoon and towed back to Chatham, and the Medway Queen Preservation Society was formed a year after that. (John Swatten)

Tahilla, Brown Owl, Fermain V and *Elvin* moored up in Dunkirk's Watier ship lock, with *Dowager* about to come alongside, during the 2010 Return. (ADLS archive)

L'ORAGE   LONDON

In 2008, HRH Prince Michael of Kent GCVO accepted an invitation to become the Honorary Admiral of the Association of Dunkirk Little Ships. This photograph shows him talking to the owners of *L'Orage* in Dunkirk during the 2010 Return. (ADLS archive)

Wairakei II leading other Little Ships out of Dunkirk soon after sunrise in 2010. (Ray Little)

Tom Tit, Hilfranor, Maid Marion, Elvin and others during the 2010 Return. (Ray Little)

On 3 June 2012, 670 vessels of an extraordinary variety took part in the Thames Diamond Jubilee Pageant to celebrate the Queen's sixty years on the throne. This fleet included forty-one Dunkirk Little Ships, some of which are seen here approaching Battersea Rail Bridge. (ADLS archive)

Sundowner leads *Lazy Days* and other Little Ships away from Battersea Rail Bridge. (John Tough)

Devon Belle leads *Mada, Wanda* and *Latona* past HMS *Belfast,* towards Tower Bridge. (Mary Ann Barton)

Little Ships have taken part in various other historic Thames events in the past: five boats moored near the Tower of London in 1967 to welcome *Gipsy Moth IV* and Sir Francis Chichester on the day he was knighted at Greenwich after he became the first person to sail single-handed round the world with just one stop; many more attended the Silver Jubilee Pageant in 1977, Tower Bridge's 100th anniversary in 1994 and the recreation of Nelson's funeral procession in 2005, among other events. This photograph shows *MTB102* passing County Hall during the Jubilee Pageant in 2012. (Bruce Gordon-Smith)

Brown Owl (formerly *Wairakei* – built 1928 and pictured here at the Jubilee Pageant) has been owned by Roger and Jennefer Balson since 1998 and she is based at Teddington. (Capture The Event)

Latona (built 1938), *Sundowner* and other Little Ships pass the London Eye during the Jubilee Pageant. After Operation Dynamo, *Latona's* contribution to the war effort continued when she was used by commandos during training exercises. (Bruce Gordon-Smith)

Many people will remember the miserable weather during the Jubilee Pageant, but the previous day was much brighter, as this photograph of *Tom Tit* moored ahead of *Mary Jane*, *L'Orage*, *Brown Owl* and *MTB102* in Barn Elms Reach shows. (John Tough)

Breda (formerly *Dab II* – built 1931) definitely went over to Dunkirk three times, and possibly four. The last time, she brought back some Dutch soldiers whose home was Breda in Holland. She continued to serve during the remainder of the war, and when her owner got her back he decided that the name *Dab II* was no longer suitable for her. He got over his superstition about changing it by retaining all the letters in the new one, which poignantly commemorates the Dutch troops she had saved. (ADLS archive)

Ken and Marion Stocks bought *Gay Venture* (built 1938) in 1990 and their daughter Heather has owned her since 2003. At that time, the boat was in a state of disrepair and may well have been scrapped, but Heather decided to use an inheritance to save her. So she took her to Michael Dennett Boat Builders and, during the course of the work, she got to know Stephen Dennett (who is now the proprietor of the yard) and soon afterwards she married him. They now have two children and they keep *Gay Venture* at Laleham Boatyard, Chertsey. These photographs show *Gay Venture* on sea trials at Hampton in 1938, and coming back from the 2010 Return. (Above: Heather Dennett collection, below: Ray Little)

Lazy Days (built 1930) spent three days at Dunkirk, ferrying troops from the beaches to ships waiting offshore. She has been owned by Kevin Finn and his family since 2013. (The Finn collection)

Vere (built 1905) is credited with saving 346 men during the Dunkirk evacuation, almost certainly by ferrying them from the beaches to outlying ships. Her current owner, Ian Campbell, bought her in 2007 after she had spent forty years in the Chichester Canal, gradually falling into a state of disrepair. During subsequent restoration work carried out in Cowes, several bullet holes and two actual bullets were found in her hull. (The King archive)

Challenge (built 1931) was one of around fifty steam-powered tugs which took part in Operation Dynamo. On 1 June she and six others received orders 'to proceed over as far as possible to Dunkirk and pick up anything'. On one occasion, a barge she had been towing was blown out of the water by a dive bomber as soon as she had released it. Later in the war, she helped tow the defensive Maunsel Towers out to the Thames Estuary and parts of the Mulberry harbour to the Normandy beaches. She is one of a number of Little Ships that would probably not have survived but for the work of the Dunkirk Little Ships Restoration Trust and a grant from the Heritage Lottery Fund. She has recently been fully restored and is based in Southampton. (Above: ADLS archive, below: Ray Little)

Humber Keels were sailing barges with square rigs but *Gainsborough Trader* (built 1931) was the first to have an engine as well, a Kelvin four-cylinder diesel. The first photograph shows her towing a sailing Keel on the Trent at Gainsborough in about 1935. Not long after that she was purchased by Pickfords, who took her to the Thames to work as a lighter. She was one of five Pickfords vessels to take part in Operation Dynamo. After ferrying troops from the shore to off-lying ships, she collected 140 more from the East Mole – she was the last non-service vessel to leave there – and brought them home. The second photograph shows her passing County Hall during the Thames Diamond Jubilee Pageant. Her current owner lives on board her at Greenland Dock in London. (Above: Humber Keel and Sloop Preservation Society archive, below: Bruce Gordon-Smith)

Every non-Return year, the ADLS organises a Commemorative Cruise to places in south-east England that were significant for the Little Ships. These photographs show *Tom Tit* and *Hilfranor* off Broadstairs on their way to Ramsgate in 2011. (John Tough)

Jockette II (built 1938) was another boat to be abandoned in 1940, in the middle of the Channel, but she was later found and towed back by a naval vessel. She has attended eight Returns and since 1964 has been in the ownership of the Gingell family, who keep her at Staines. (Jose Bermudez collection)

Count Dracula (built 1913) might be considered to be poacher-turned-gamekeeper. She was built for the German Imperial Navy, and somehow survived into private British ownership when the German fleet was scuttled at Scapa Flow in 1918. During Operation Dynamo, she ferried more than 700 troops from the beaches to larger vessels waiting offshore, and then picked up thirty-eight Royal Engineers – just as they were exchanging fire with advancing German forces – and brought them back to Ramsgate. (ADLS archive)

This photograph shows the two boats that have attended the most Returns: *L'Orage* has been to all of them, while *Thamesa* has only missed 2005, when she blew a cylinder head gasket. (ADLS archive)

Every Little Ship that attends a Dunkirk Return is presented with a commemorative plaque. This photograph, taken soon after the 2000 Return, shows *L'Orage*'s impressive collection. (Ray Little)

Thamesa, Tom Tit and *Lazy Days* entering Ramsgate Harbour after the 2010 Return. While crossing to Dunkirk in 1940, *Tom Tit* (built 1938) briefly went aground while her crew fixed a petrol leak, but when they got there she made sixteen trips ferrying men to outlying ships. She eventually left just as German troops were arriving on the Mole. (Ray Little)

Janthea and *Gay Venture* on the 2010 Return. Both these boats were built in 1938. (ADLS archive)

To commemorate the 70th anniversary of the liberation of Ostend, seventeen Little Ships – including *Caronia* (built 1927) – attended the annual 'Ostend At Anchor' event in 2014. *Caronia* was in Le Havre when war broke out and fled quickly home, but it wasn't long before she was back on the French coast taking part in Operation Dynamo. She has been owned by Peter Draper since 2002. He and his son Lewis spent a great deal of time restoring her between the 2005 and 2010 Returns and plan to offer charters in her from their base in Chichester harbour. (ADLS archive)

Iorana (built 1935) is one of many Little Ships about whose Dunkirk service very little is known, which is hardly surprising considering the manner and speed in which such a vast number of vessels were commandeered and sent into action. She is pictured here on her way from Ramsgate to the 'Ostend At Anchor' event in 2014. (Alex Ramsay)

NEW BRITANNIC, RAMSGATE.
THE LITTLE BOAT THAT WENT TO DUNKIRK,
SKIPPER; W. READ.

The *New Britannic* (built 1930) spent two days at Dunkirk and is credited with ferrying around 3,000 men out to waiting ships and bringing eighty-three more back to Ramsgate. Her skipper was Walter Read, whose fifteen-year-old son Joe – thought to be the youngest person to take part in the evacuation – was also on board. She is another boat that would probably not survive today without the intervention of the Dunkirk Little Ships Restoration Trust. These photographs show her leaving Ramsgate on a pleasure trip in the 1950s (above, Sheila Johnson collection), and attending the 'Ostend At Anchor' event in 2014 (below, ADLS archive).

The Thames Traditional Boat Rally is another event regularly attended by the Little Ships. This photograph shows a number of them, with the Lancaster from the Battle of Britain Memorial Flight overhead, in 2010. (Ray Little)

Gay Venture, Monarch, Wanda and *Lurline* at the Thames Traditional Boat Rally in 2005. Sadly, *Monarch* has since been broken up. (Ray Little)

The voyage that the *Devon Belle* (formerly *Seymour Castle* – built 1938) made to Dover to take part in Operation Dynamo was much the longest she had ever made, having been built in Dartmouth as a River Dart passenger vessel. She performs the same role today, but at Caversham, in the ownership of Thames River Cruises. She is pictured above in 2008 at the Thames Traditional Boat Rally (with a Lancaster approaching overhead); and below leading *Greta*, *Gainsborough Trader*, *Stenoa* and the Ramsgate lifeboat *Esme Anderson* across to Dunkirk in 2005. (Ray Little)

In the mid-1980s the then-owner of *Naiad Errant*, Sandy Evans, instigated a new annual event for the Little Ships: the Veterans' Cruise. While it was initially just for Dunkirk veterans, other Second World War veterans were later included. However, it is a sad but inevitable fact that, as the years passed, fewer and fewer of them were able to attend, and so veterans from more recent conflicts are now invited. The event takes place on the Thames between Teddington and Shepperton over the first weekend of September and typically about twenty Little Ships take part. Saturday is for veterans of later conflicts and finishes with a dinner at Thames Motor Yacht Club, while Sunday is for Second World War veterans, who are taken to Weybridge Mariners Club for lunch. These photographs show the fleet assembling in Teddington Barge Lock, with *MTB102* leading the way in 2012, above; and *Lady Gay* and *L'Orage* bringing up the rear in Molesey Lock in 2014, below. (ADLS archive)

Mada (formerly *Fleury II* – built 1936) at the 2014 Veterans' Cruise, with veterans from the South Atlantic Medal Association and ratings from HMS *Collingwood*, Victory Squadron. (ADLS archive)

Papillon (built 1930) taking part in the 2014 Veterans' Cruise. She is owned by Ian Gilbert – the Commodore of the ADLS and the organiser of the Veterans' Cruises since the late 2000s – and his wife Karina, and kept on the Thames at Weybridge. (ADLS archive)

White Marlin, Gay Venture and *Chumley* waiting to go upstream through Moseley Lock on the Veterans' Cruise in 2014. The Veterans' Cruises also pass through Sunbury Lock. (ADLS archive)

Tom Tit at the 2014 Veterans' Cruise, with Royal Navy ratings from HMS *Collingwood*, Victory Squadron. (ADLS archive)

Riis I at the Veterans' Cruise in 2014. (ADLS archive)

Lady Gay with *White Marlin* and *Aureol* at the 2014 Veterans' Cruise. *White Marlin* (formerly *Fervant*) went straight from her builder's yard into naval service when she was completed in 1939. During Operation Dynamo, she was subjected to sustained air attacks as she got close to Dunkirk. Although she wasn't hit, her engines were damaged and she turned round and limped home at a much reduced speed. (ADLS archive)

Lady Gay, with Second World War veterans and Chelsea Pensioners, leaving Molesey Lock to head upstream in 2014; and arriving at Ramsgate for the 2010 Return. (Above: ADLS archive, below: Ian Gilbert)

Wairakei II was built in 1932 for an owner who had previously had *Brown Owl*, another Dunkirk Little Ship. These photographs show her at the 2014 Veterans' Cruise, and in Paris many years ago. She is now based in London. (ADLS archive)

Elizabeth Green (built 1935) went over to Dunkirk twice in 1940. During the first trip, she towed whalers full of troops out to ships waiting offshore, transferred the crew of a boat with a fouled propeller to a minesweeper, and then returned to Ramsgate with a full load of men. She set off again under tow a few days later, but when the tow rope broke she made her own way across. She went alongside a quay in Dunkirk harbour and embarked about twenty French soldiers with the help of a ladder she had taken across, and brought them back to Sheerness. She is pictured here when she was owned by John Knight. (ADLS archive)

Marsayru (built 1937) took part in Operation Dynamo for at least three days. She ferried troops from the beaches and is credited with rescuing about 400, nineteen of which she brought back to Ramsgate. On the first night, she came adrift when under tow and was lost in the darkness, but she was found empty by a naval pinnace the following morning. The next day, she was machine-gunned by four German planes but escaped unscathed. She is pictured here with her original owners in Rochester, probably in 1938, and she is now owned by David and Trish Shotton. (John Humphreys collection)

Two contrasting photographs of *Silver Queen*: at Barry Island in 1927, the year after she was built; and at Royal Victoria Dock, where she now operates as a charter vessel, in 2014. (Joe Radmore collection)

Bibliography

www.dunkirk-revisited.co.uk, by John Richards

Divine, A. D., *Dunkirk* (London: Faber & Faber Ltd, 1945)

Brann, Christian, *The Little Ships of Dunkirk* (Cirencester: Collectors' Books Ltd, 1989)

de Winser, John S., *BEF Ships Before, At and After Dunkirk*, (Gravesend: World Ship Society, 1999)

Plummer, Russell, *The Ships That Saved An Army*, (Patrick Stephens Ltd (Thorsons Publishing Group), 1990)

Yachting World (London: Time Inc. (UK) Ltd)

Motor Boat and Yachting (London: Time Inc. (UK) Ltd)

Yachting Monthly (London: Time Inc. (UK) Ltd)